IMAGES
of America

FORT McHENRY
AND BALTIMORE'S
HARBOR DEFENSES

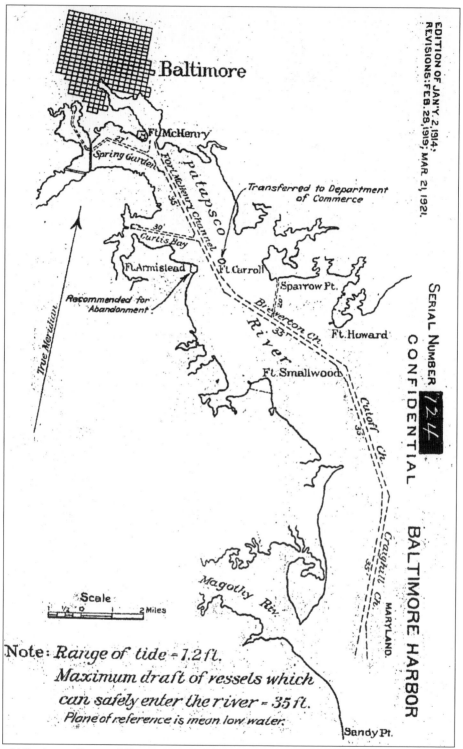

Baltimore

Ft. McHenry

Spring Garden

Patapsco

Fort McHenry Channel

Transferred to Department
of Commerce

Curtis Bay

Ft. Armistead

Ft. Carroll

Sparrow Pt.

Recommended for
Abandonment

Bewerton Ch.

Ft. Howard

River

Ft. Smallwood

True Meridian

Cutoff Ch.

Craighill Cr.

Magothy Riv.

Scale

1 ½ 0 2 Miles

Sandy Pt.

Note: Range of tide = 1.2 ft.
Maximum draft of vessels which
can safely enter the river = 35 ft.
Plane of reference is mean low water.

This U.S. Army Corps of Engineers map shows Baltimore Harbor channels and forts as of March 21, 1921. (Courtesy of National Archives.)

IMAGES
of America

FORT McHENRY
AND BALTIMORE'S
HARBOR DEFENSES

Merle T. Cole and Scott S. Sheads

ARCADIA

First printed 2001
Reprinted 2003

Published by Arcadia Publishing
Charleston SC, Chicago IL, Portsmouth NH, San Francisco CA

Printed in Great Britain

Library of Congress Catalog Card Number: 2001088669

For all general information contact Arcadia Publishing at
Telephone 843-853-2070
Fax 843-853-0044
E-Mail sales@arcadiapublishing.com
For customer service and orders:
Toll-Free 1-888-313-2665

Visit us on the internet at http://www.arcadiapublishing.com

CONTENTS

ACKNOWLEDGMENTS

The authors gratefully acknowledge the assistance provided by Bolling W. Smith and Mark A. Berhow of the Coast Defense Study Group, Inc., and Eleanor Lukanich of the Dundalk-Patapsco Neck Historical Society.

INTRODUCTION

The harbor defenses of Baltimore present a unique example of United States coastal fortification. An earthen fort built at Whetstone Point during the Revolutionary War was never attacked, but the location proved excellent because it was situated at the tip of a peninsula far enough from central Baltimore to provide protection without endangering the city. Enemy vessels could not approach Baltimore without passing Whetstone Point. Fort McHenry was constructed there between 1799 and 1802. A brick fort in the shape of a five-pointed star, it was named after Secretary of War James McHenry, who had been instrumental in raising funds for its construction.

The Royal Navy finally did attack Baltimore during the War of 1812. Soldiers, sailors, and Royal Marines, fresh from victory at Bladensburg and the burning of Washington, debarked at North Point on the morning of September 12, 1814. Their mission was to march up Patapsco Neck and capture Baltimore from the east. Maryland militia under Brig. Gen. John Stricker were ordered to delay the invaders, buying time for completion of entrenchments being frantically dug around the city. In the Battle of North Point the militiamen conducted a successful delaying action then fell back to the trench lines. The British, exhausted by the fighting, surprised by the militia's firm resistance, and confronted with a formidable set of entrenchments, retraced their steps and reembarked at North Point.

Fort McHenry and several earthen batteries guarded the water approach to Baltimore. To cover the land attack, Royal Navy ships began bombarding Fort McHenry on September 13. The mixed American force of regulars and militia under Maj. George Armistead withstood 25 hours of artillery and rocket fire, while American guns kept the British at a distance. With the failure of the land assault and bombardment, the British departed. While observing the bombardment Francis Scott Key was inspired to write "The Star-Spangled Banner," later adopted as the national anthem.

During the Civil War, Union troops were stationed at Fort McHenry as part of the occupying force that kept Maryland from seceding. The fort's guns were turned toward the city, and the fort was used as a prison for civilians—including Maryland legislators—suspected of Confederate sympathies, as well as captured Confederate soldiers.

During World War I the War Department established General Hospital No. 2 at Fort McHenry in 1919. It was the largest military hospital in the country, with over 100 temporary buildings housing American soldiers wounded in Europe. After the war the need for the hospital slowly diminished, and on March 3, 1925, Fort McHenry was transferred to the

National Park Service. It is the country's sole National Monument and Historic Shrine, being so designated on August 11, 1939.

Fort McHenry was an administrative rather than a combat post following the Civil War. The capture of Fort Pulaski, Georgia, during that war had convincingly demonstrated that brick forts were unable to resist fire from new rifled heavy artillery. As armored warships became common following the famous *Monitor-Merrimac* duel, the value of smoothbore artillery declined, while increased range of naval ordnance mandated that harbor forts be located further away from the sites they protected.

Baltimore's only other permanent costal fortification, Fort Carroll, had been constructed on an artificial island in the Patapsco River during 1847–1868. It was named in 1850 for Charles Carroll, the only living signer of the Declaration of Independence. The principal project engineer was Capt. Robert E. Lee.

Despite technological advancements, the United States, wearied by the Civil War, was slow to examine its coastal fortification needs. Baltimore became acutely aware of its vulnerability to naval attack in late 1873, when war with Spain appeared imminent because of the *Virginius* affair. Relationships deteriorated to the point that President Grant had ordered the Navy mobilized before diplomats averted war. All that could be done in Baltimore was to "mount one fifteen-inch smooth-bore gun at Fort Carroll and to renovate the old water battery at [Fort] McHenry." The only other effective defensive measure would have been to sink old hulks in the channel, but this would also have blocked much of Baltimore's commercial traffic.

Efforts to modernize America's seacoast defenses languished until 1886, when a committee chaired by Secretary of War William C. Endicott presented a detailed corrective plan incorporating newly emerging weapon systems. Although technology quickly surpassed the Endicott Board recommendations, the basic scheme was retained for the next 30 years. Defenses based on the committee report are referred to as Endicott Era works.

U.S. Army plans for modernizing Baltimore's defenses changed markedly, but eventually settled on erecting new artillery batteries at Rock Point, Hawkins Point, and North Point; installing modern armament atop Fort Carroll; and providing extensive minefields to close navigable channels to enemy warships (see map on page 2). The necessary land was obtained through condemnation proceedings but progress was otherwise very slow. Although Congress sanctioned the Endicott Board's plan, it provided little in the way of appropriations until 1896, when increasing tensions with Spain over Cuba prompted the largest outlay for fortifications in the country's history up to that time. Frantic, round-the-clock construction of harbor defenses began in early 1898, spurred by fears of Spanish Navy raids on eastern seaboard cities. Severe weather hampered work at Baltimore during January and February, but the Army still made good use of a last minute $50 million congressional appropriation for national defense.

The Spanish-American War lasted from April to August 1898. During the course of the "splendid little war" only a handful of the planned artillery pieces were actually mounted in the Baltimore defenses—one 12-inch and three 8-inch guns at Hawkins Point, and eight 12-inch mortars at North Point. The city depended primarily on submarines mines for protection. These were laid along the channel from Fort McHenry to a point a half-mile below Fort Carroll. The channels were kept open for shipping but extra mines were kept ashore to be promptly planted should Spanish warships enter Chesapeake Bay. Despite Army assurances, fear of accidentally detonating mines caused Baltimore's waterborne commerce to slack off that summer. The belligerents signed a peace protocol on August 12, and the War Department quickly ordered the mines removed. Because the mines had been filled with loose dynamite, it was wisely decided to detonate them "in place."

Mounting artillery in the new emplacements along the Patapsco continued until 1905, by which date the War Department had officially named the reservations and individual batteries (see table). One fort and five batteries were named for heroes of the 1814 defense. As noted above, Major Armistead commanded the Fort McHenry garrison and General Stricker the militia at North Point. Judge Joseph H. Nicholson was a captain of Volunteer Artillery at Fort

McHenry where Lt. Levi Clagett was killed during the bombardment. Col. David Harris commanded a regiment of Baltimore artillery, and Key authored the "Star-Spangled Banner." The other forts and batteries were named for various heroes of the Revolutionary, 1812, Seminole, Mexican, Civil, and Spanish-American Wars, and the Philippine Insurrection. The exception was Battery Lazear, named in honor of Dr. Jesse W. Lazear, a Baltimore physician who died attempting to eradicate yellow fever in Cuba.

Location, Designation, and Armament of Endicott Era Defenses of Baltimore Harbor

Fort/Location	Battery	Armament
Fort Howard, North Point	Key	eight 12-inch breechloading mortars
	Stricker	two 12-inch breechloading rifles
	Nicholson	two 6-inch breechloading rifles
	Harris	two 5-inch rapid fire guns
	Lazear	two 5-inch rapid fire guns
	Clagett	two 3-inch rapid fire guns
Fort Carroll, Sollers Point Flats	Towson	two 12-inch breechloading rifles
	Heart	two 5-inch rapid fire guns
	Augustin	two 3-inch rapid fire guns
Fort Armistead, Hawkins Point	Winchester	one 12-inch breechloading rifle
	McFarland	three 8-inch breechloading rifles
	Irons	two 4.7-inch rapid fire guns
	Mudge	two 3-inch rapid fire guns
Fort Smallwood, Rock Point	Hartshorne	two 6-inch breechloading rifles
	Sykes	two 3-inch rapid fire guns

It is difficult to appreciate today that harbor defense was the Army's high-technology, "Star Wars" branch at the turn of the century. In the days before radio, radar, and aircraft, when the telephone was little beyond its infancy, coast artillery employed complex, sophisticated weapons systems in a demanding mission—destroying and damaging heavily armored, moving warships at long ranges. Long hours spent in training helped assure the needed precise execution.

Under a 1907 concentration plan, 32 of the 78 coast defense forts having modern armaments were designated main posts to be manned as fully as Coast Artillery Corps strength allowed. The remaining forts were designated subposts and manned only by caretaker detachments. Fort Howard became the main post for Baltimore with four companies assigned, while Forts Carroll, Armistead, and Smallwood were each cared for by a single electrician-sergeant.

None of Baltimore's Endicott Era forts saw combat. In World War I the German fleet was blockaded by the Royal Navy. The Coast Artillery Corps largely manned garrisons against the possibility of small-scale raids by individual enemy warships and trained heavy and trench artillerymen for service overseas. Fort Howard served as a major training center. Included among the students were men from the Maryland National Guard's 1st Coast Artillery Battalion. Further reflecting the absence of a serious enemy threat to the continental United States, artillery pieces were dismounted from several Baltimore batteries, intended for shipment overseas.

Just as technological progress had brought Baltimore's Endicott defenses into being, it caused their demise. Once ordnance powerful enough to block the entrance to the Chesapeake had been installed at Cape Henry there was no longer a need for harbor forts inside the bay, and the War Department decided to discontinue Baltimore's harbor defenses. Dismounted artillery pieces were not reinstalled, and by the end of December 1920 Coast Artillery Corps personnel had been transferred from Fort Howard to Fort Monroe. A single company was assigned to Fort Howard from 1922 to 1927, when the remaining coast artillery ordnance was removed.

Fort Howard continued as an active Army post, housing the Third Corps Area headquarters, an infantry brigade headquarters, and part of an infantry regiment. The installation hosted a Citizens' Military Training Camp in the 1920s and a Civilian Conservation Corps camp in the 1930s. Fort Howard was transferred to the Veterans Administration by presidential executive order on August 2, 1940. Some 60 acres in the battery area were transferred to the U.S. Army Intelligence School at Fort Holabird in 1956, and soldiers deploying to Southeast Asia trained at a simulated Vietnamese village constructed there. This land was transferred to Baltimore County in November 1973 for use as a waterfront park.

The Army sold Fort Armistead to Baltimore city in 1927, but the reservation was again used by the military during World War II (for Navy ammunition storage) and in the early days of the Cold War (as an Army antiaircraft artillery site) before reverting to its present role as a city park. Fort Smallwood was sold to the city and has remained a park since 1927. Fort Carroll remained federal property until 1958, when it was sold to a private owner.

One
THE ROCKETS' RED GLARE

This 1882 marble monument to Colonel Armistead rests atop Federal Hill overlooking the Baltimore waterfront. (Courtesy of National Park Service.)

Col. James McHenry was secretary of war under both George Washington and John Adams. The fort at Whetstone Point was named in his honor in 1797. (Courtesy of National Park Service.)

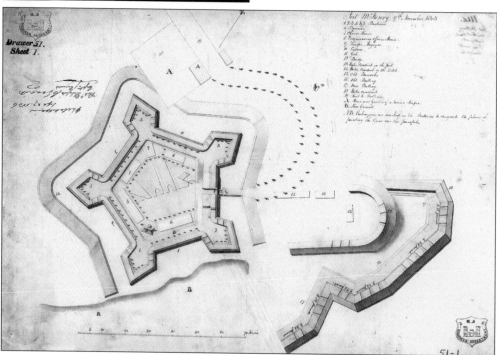

An 1806 map of Fort McHenry shows the outer batteries and famous star fort design soon after its completion. Seven years later more improvements were made by engineers to confront a British threat to Baltimore. (Courtesy of National Park Service.)

An 1810 view shows Whetstone Point with the seaport of Fells Point in the foreground. Fort McHenry is located within the trees at the tip of the peninsula. (Courtesy of National Park Service.)

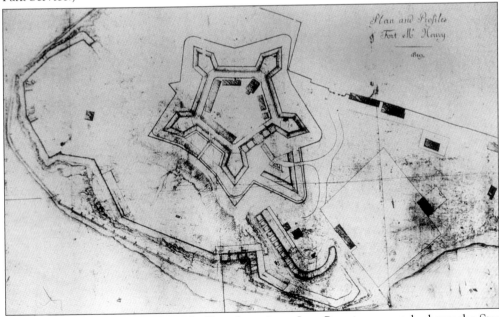

An 1819 "plan and profile" drawn by French engineer Jean Poussin accurately shows the Star Fort much as it appeared during the famous bombardment of 1814. Two tiers of water batteries mounting 36 naval guns, the main harbor defense of Baltimore, can be seen at the bottom. Many of America's early coastal fortifications were designed and constructed by European engineers. (Courtesy of National Archives.)

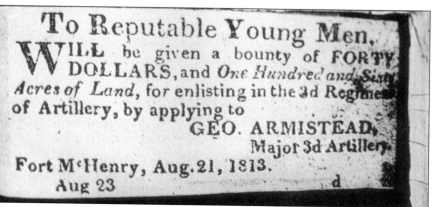

To Reputable Young Men,

WILL be given a bounty of FORTY DOLLARS, and *One Hundred and Sixty Acres of Land*, for enlisting in the 3d Regiment of Artillery, by applying to

GEO. ARMISTEAD,
Major 3d Artillery.

Fort M'Henry, Aug. 21, 1813.
Aug 23   d

A recruitment notice was placed in the Baltimore newspapers during August of 1813 by Major Armistead to enlist citizens in the 3rd Regiment, U.S. Artillery, the regular Fort McHenry garrison. (Courtesy of National Park Service.)

THE FENCIBLES

ARE hereby notified, that, for very urgent reasons, it has been found necessary to change the original plan of organizing a company of infantry, and a considerable majority of the company have determined to attach themselves to the artillery, it is hoped that this determination will be unanimously concurred in.

Certificates of membership are now ready to be delivered on application to the secretary, Mr. James L. Hawkins, at the Commercial & Farmers Bank.

Swords are to be procured at Mr. James C. Neilson's or Mr. Walraven's. *Belts & Knapsacks* at Mr. J. M'Cabe's near Gadsby's.

☞ You will assemble for drill, at Clemm's lot, on THURSDAY next, the 29th inst. completely equipt, at 4 o'clock.

JOSEPH NICHOLSON, Captain.
april 23   d lt

Also in 1813, Capt. Joseph H. Nicholson placed this notice to recruit members for the Baltimore Fencibles, U.S. Volunteers, who helped defend Fort McHenry during the War of 1812. Nicholson was a well-known judge of the Circuit Court of Appeals of Maryland who raised this artillery company from among Baltimore merchants. (Courtesy of National Park Service.)

The Aquilla Randall Monument is located near the site of the Battle of North Point. One face is inscribed as follows: "In the skirmish which occurred at this spot between the advanced party under Major Richard Heath of the 5th Regiment, Maryland Militia and the front of the British column, Major General Robert Ross the commander of the British force received his mortal wound." (Courtesy of National Park Service.)

Here is the site of the Old Methodist Meeting House on the North Point battleground, where the wounded from the two-hour battle on September 12, 1814 were cared for prior to the bombardment of Fort McHenry the next day. A 1914 commemorative stone marker marks the site. (Courtesy of National Park Service.)

An early 19th-century watercolor shows the site where Maj. Gen. Robert Ross, commander of the British land forces during the Battle of North Point, was mortally wounded on September 12, 1814. A monument marks the site today. (Courtesy of National Park Service.)

A roadside marker at Old North Point designates where British General Ross was mortally wounded by American sharpshooters. (Courtesy of Scott S. Sheads.)

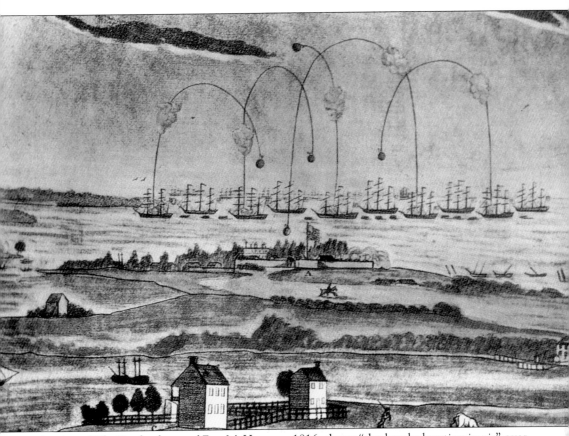

A print of *The Bombardment of Fort McHenry, c.* 1816, shows "the bombs bursting in air" over the ramparts. It was the most popular contemporary view of the battle and was widely circulated during the 19th century. (Courtesy of National Park Service.)

Kenneth Townsend's 1989 painting of the Fort McHenry bombardment depicts the British fleet firing from two miles down the Patapsco. (Courtesy of National Park Service.)

Pictured here is one of the many African Americans who helped defend Baltimore and Washington during the War of 1812. This is an artist's depiction of Charles Ball, an able seaman of the U.S. Chesapeake Flotilla, who in 1836 wrote his memoirs, *The Life and Adventures of Charles Ball*. (Courtesy of National Park Service.)

Fort Covington, seen here in an 1819 plan, was named for Brig. Gen. Leonard Covington, a Marylander killed in Upper Canada during the War of 1812. The fort was located in South Baltimore and guarded the western water approaches to Baltimore and Fort McHenry. On the night of September 13, 1814, the garrison of sailors from USS *Guerriere* thwarted an attempted British shore assault. (Courtesy of National Archives.)

In 1816 the citizens of Baltimore presented this 13-inch silver punch bowl with goblets and a serving tray to Colonel Armistead for his gallant defense of Fort McHenry. The bowl was made in the shape of a British mortar shell. Today it is exhibited at the Smithsonian Museum of American History along with the original Star-Spangled Banner. (Courtesy of National Park Service.)

BATTLE MONUMENT.

The Corner Stone of which was laid in Baltimore at the Solemnity of the 12th of Sept. 1815. in Commemoration of the Defenders of this City who fell on the XII of Sept. 1814. at the Battle of North Point & the XIII during the Bombardment of Fort McHenry.

The 1815 Battle Monument in downtown Baltimore commemorates the defense of Fort McHenry and the Battle of North Point during the War of 1812. Lt. Col. George Armistead, the commander of Fort McHenry, laid the cornerstone of what became in 1827 the official emblem of the City of Baltimore. (Courtesy of National Park Service.)

A rare group portrait of the "Old Defenders," *c.* 1873, shows veterans who fought to protect Baltimore during the War of 1812. (Courtesy of National Park Service.)

Two
CIVIL WAR CITADEL

FORT Mc HENRY, BALTIMORE, Mᴅ

A popular 1862 E. Sasche & Co. print shows Fort McHenry when the 2nd U.S. Artillery garrisoned the post. In the foreground are the gate and wall constructed in 1837. (Courtesy of National Park Service.)

A schooner passes Fort McHenry during the Civil War. In the background the officers' quarters and the sally port (left) are visible. (Courtesy of National Park Service.)

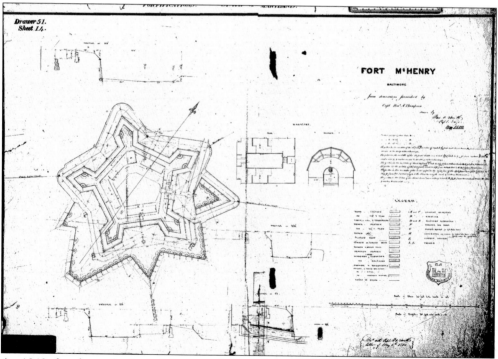

An 1840 plan shows the fort's defenses and the outline of the powder magazine shortly after the U.S. Army upgraded the fort from the War of 1812 period. (Courtesy of National Park Service.)

The Pratt Street Riot of April 19, 1861, occurred when an angry mob of Southern sympathizers attacked the 6th Massachusetts Regiment as it passed through Baltimore on its way to Washington. The riot inspired James Ryder Randall, a young Marylander then residing in New Orleans, to write "Maryland, My Maryland," which became the official state song in 1939. (Courtesy of National Park Service.)

An 1861 watercolor view of Fort McHenry outbuildings shows the officers' quarters and seawall. (Courtesy of National Archives.)

The fort viewed from the Patapsco River at sunset was illustrated in *Harpers Weekly* on May 11, 1861. (Courtesy of National Park Service.)

An artist's view of Fort McHenry in July 1861 shows the 34-star garrison flag waving proudly over the ramparts. (Courtesy of National Park Service.)

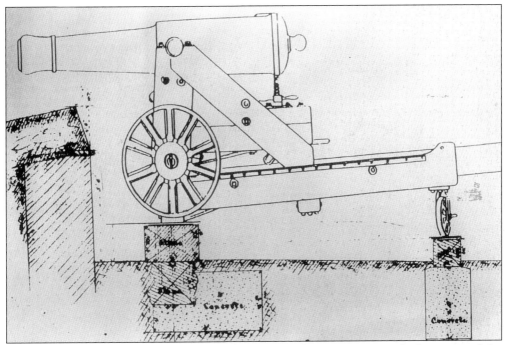

This drawing illustrates one of the Model 1842 32-pounder seacoast guns which comprised the fort's principal armament during the Civil War. This particular gun site (No. 8) is still located on Bastion No. 4 of the Star Fort (see photo below). (Courtesy of National Park Service.)

In one of only two known photographs of fort armament taken during the Civil War, Gun No. 8 on Bastion No. 4 looks out across the Patapsco River. Beyond this gun the outer batteries are visible. (Courtesy of National Park Service.)

Brig. Gen. Benjamin Butler commanded the Union force that occupied Federal Hill on the night of May 13, 1861. This action "captured" Baltimore and secured it for the Union for the remainder of the Civil War. (Courtesy of National Archives.)

Maj. Gen.George Cadwalader commanded the Military Department of Maryland in May 1861 when his three Pennsylvania regiments occupied Locust Point just outside the gates of Fort McHenry. That same month Cadwalader refused a writ of *habeas corpus* from U.S. Chief Justice Roger Brooke Taney for civilian John Merryman, whom Cadwalader detained at the fort. This case aroused wide debate over the constitutional rights of citizens arrested without due process of law. (Courtesy of National Park Service.)

This second-floor piazza of the barracks inside the Star Fort is where members of the Maryland Legislature were imprisoned in September 1861 to prevent their possible vote for secession. One Maryland politician described the fort as "a chicken-coup of a garrison." (Courtesy of National Park Service.)

A 1905 view shows the historic sally port. On either side of the entrance are cells where members of the Maryland Legislature were detained in 1861. (Courtesy of National Park Service.)

The Union encampment at the fort is seen here in 1862. In the foreground of this lithograph is the old 1826 Lazaretto lighthouse, which was removed in 1959. (Courtesy of National Park Service.)

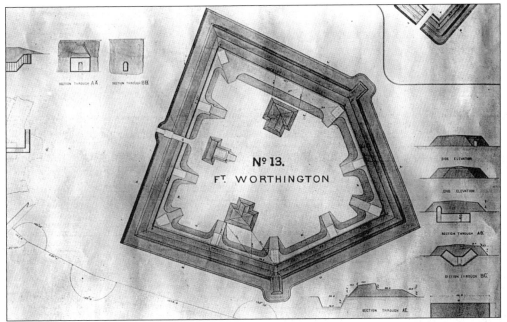

Late in the war, forts were also erected to defend Baltimore from overland attack. By mid-June 1864, Generals Grant and Lee were locked in the siege at Petersburg, Virginia. To ease Union pressure, Lee sent Maj. Gen. Jubal A. Early's corps on a raid up the Shenandoah Valley toward Washington. Early crossed the Potomac, fought at the Monocacy River on July 9, and reached Fort Stevens on the northern outskirts of Washington two days later. When reinforcements dispatched by Grant arrived, Early broke off his raid on the 12th and returned to the Valley. In response to Early's attack, 43 forts and earthen redoubts were thrown up around Baltimore in August 1864. This is the plan for Fort Worthington (Fort No. 13), which was located at Kenwood and Preston Streets and mounted nine field guns. (Courtesy of National Archives.)

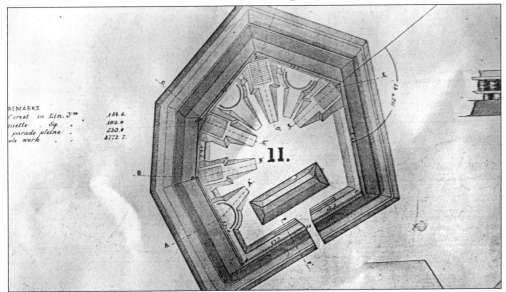

Fort No. 11 was an earthen fort constructed at Chester and Elderry Streets and mounted seven field guns. (Courtesy of National Archives.)

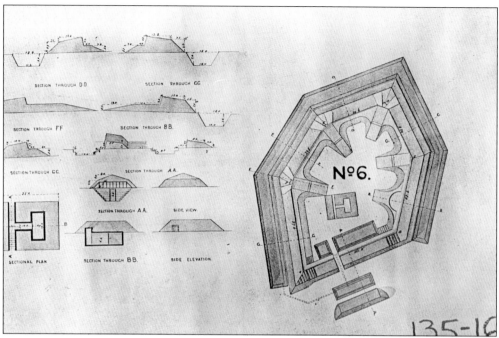

Fort No. 6 was an earthen emplacement built at Madison Avenue in Druid Hill Park. (Courtesy of National Archives.)

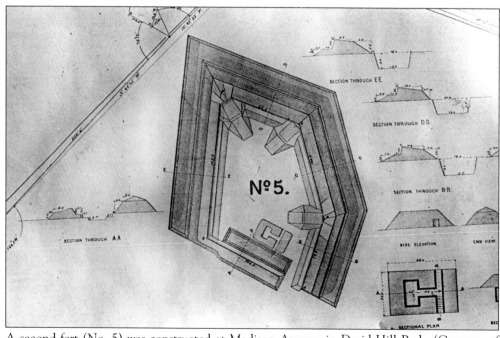

A second fort (No. 5) was constructed at Madison Avenue in Druid Hill Park. (Courtesy of National Archives.)

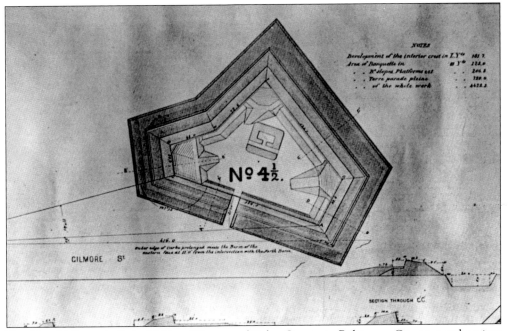

Fort No. 4 1/2 was built in 1864 at Gilmor and Baker Streets in Baltimore City to guard against a rebel attack from the west. (Courtesy of National Archives.)

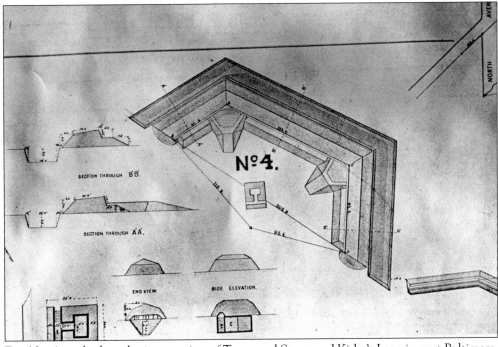

Fort No. 4 was built at the intersection of Townsend Street and Kirby's Lane in west Baltimore. (Courtesy of National Archives.)

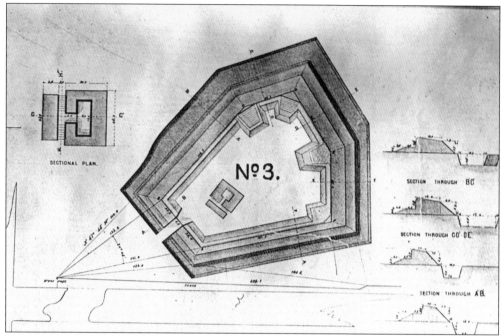

Fort No. 3—also situated at Franklin and Kirby's Lane—was defended by the loyal Union forces of Baltimore. (Courtesy of National Archives.)

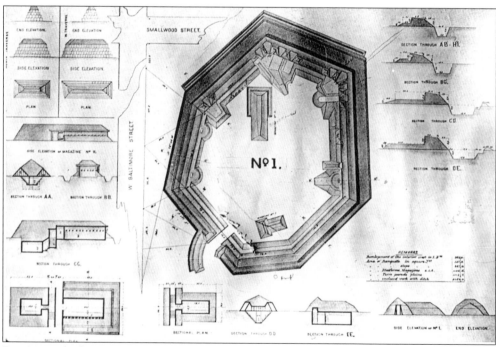

Fort No. 1, built at West Baltimore and Smallwood Streets, mounted ten field guns. (Courtesy of National Archives.)

On the afternoon of July 3, 1863, the garrison and Baltimore residents could hear artillery firing at Gettysburg, 58 miles to the north. Afterwards nearly 7,000 Confederate captives were imprisoned at the fort pending transfer to larger facilities. Many were housed in the 1843 stables (now barracks) in the background of this 1905 view of the parade ground. (Courtesy of Scott S. Sheads.)

A *c.* 1865 view shows an artillery park at Fort McHenry, with 12-pounder Napoleon field pieces and their limbers in the foreground, and unmounted Rodmans along the fence line. Officers' quarters are along the waterfront. (Courtesy of National Park Service.)

This plan, dated June 30, 1864, shows emplacements for 72 cannon and mortars that armed the fort during the Civil War. In 1866, more powerful 10-inch and 15-inch Rodman guns replaced the earlier seacoast guns used during the war. (Courtesy of National Park Service.)

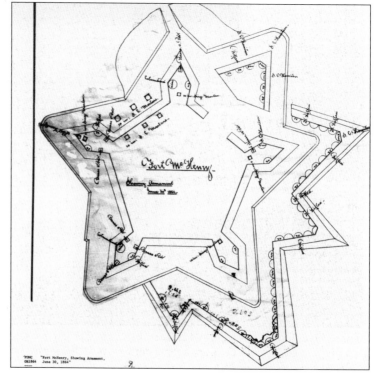

Three
THE WORLD WARS

Three biplanes fly over Fort McHenry in 1926. At left center are the 1916 immigration buildings, used by U.S. Treasury agents during the 1920s in the fight to enforce prohibition in Baltimore. (Courtesy of National Park Service.)

A tranquil scene on an 1873 Sunday afternoon takes place as visitors view the Patapsco River from the old Star Fort. Nearby is one of the five 15-inch Rodman guns mounted in 1866. Tourists often outnumbered the small garrison. (Courtesy of National Park Service.)

This view of the 1879 guardhouse was taken c. 1910. This structure was built to replace the earlier (1837) guardhouse within the Star Fort. (Courtesy of National Park Service.)

The ivy-covered stone post chapel, built in 1886, was a popular place for weddings during the later part of the 19th century. It was removed in 1927. (Courtesy of National Park Service.)

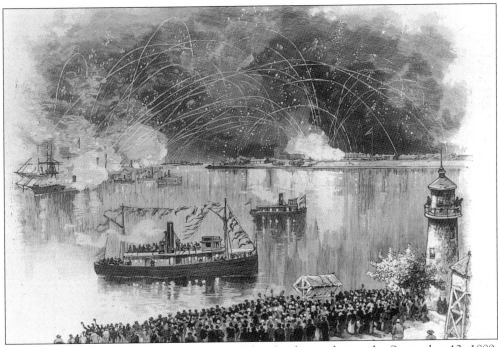

Visitors at Lazaretto Lighthouse view a mock bombardment during the September 12, 1889, Defenders' Day celebration captured in this *Harper's Weekly* illustration. A battery guarded Lazaretto Point on this site during the 1814 battle. (Courtesy of National Park Service.)

This rare portrait shows an ordnance sergeant, *c.* 1899, seated at his desk in the old ordnance building at Fort McHenry. The building is currently used by the U.S. Army Corps of Engineers, and is one of the few surviving 19th-century outbuildings on the park grounds. (Courtesy of National Park Service.)

This *c.* 1903 portrait shows the members of the 141st Company, Coastal Artillery Corps in dress uniform. The last active Coast Artillery Corps garrison departed Fort McHenry on July 12, 1912. (Courtesy of National Park Service.)

A rare photograph depicts experimental 8-inch Rodman guns firing a salute on July 3, 1903, as part of Independence Day observances. On the earthen magazine in the background officers observe the effect of firing. (Courtesy of National Park Service.)

The Rodman guns are being reloaded (above) and fired again (below). The obscurity is typical of black powder weapons. These cannons are still at the fort. (Courtesy of National Park Service.)

The c. 1905 view above shows the Star Fort's central parade ground. (Courtesy of National Park Service.)

This 1905 view shows the old junior officers quarters inside the Star Fort being used as a bakery. In 1929 the Army restored the old quarters to their 1830 appearance, complete with a second story and piazza. (Courtesy of National Park Service.)

This view looks up Fort Road to the main entrance in 1905. To the right are the enlisted barracks and pyramided stacks of cannon balls. (Courtesy of National Park Service.)

Sentries of 141st Company, Coastal Artillery Corps guard the entrance gates in 1910. Beyond this massive guardhouse, which was built in 1879, are the fort's interior grounds. In the foreground are the Fort Avenue tracks of the No. 1 streetcar line. (Courtesy of National Park Service.)

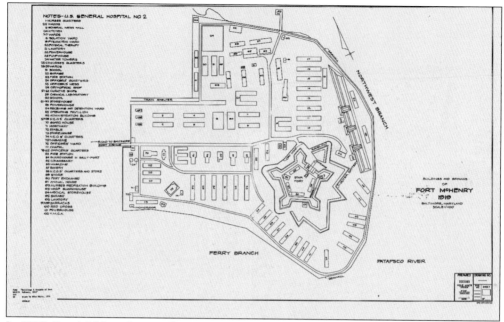

In 1919, Fort McHenry's grounds were transformed into one of the nation's largest U.S. Army hospitals to receive wounded from World War I. Eventually some 140 buildings surrounded the Star Fort. With a capacity of 3,000 beds and 1,200 medical staff, U.S. Army General Hospital No. 2 specialized in facial reconstruction and neurosurgery. This is a 1919 general plan. (Courtesy of National Park Service.)

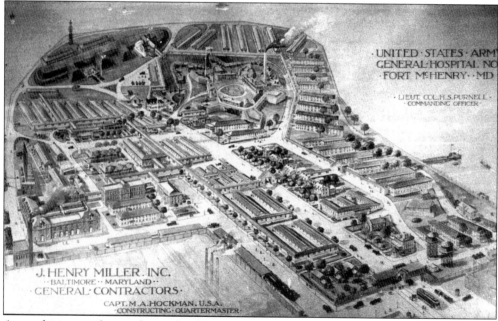

An architect rendering shows the hospital soon after its completion in 1920. Only the Receiving Station, where troop transports brought the wounded from Europe, remains today. (Courtesy of National Park Service.)

The view above shows the convalescent wards of U.S. Army General Hospital No. 2. (Courtesy of National Park Service.)

Hospital trucks are seen here parked alongside the fort walls in 1920. (Courtesy of National Park Service.)

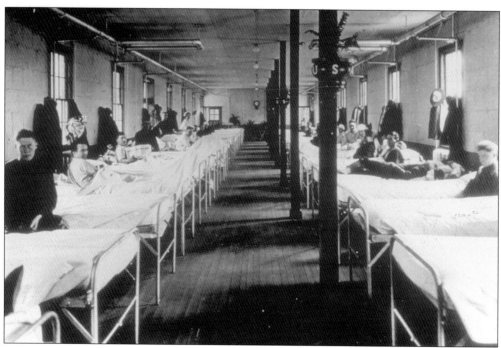

An interior view shows one of the 20 convalescent wards. (Courtesy of National Park Service.)

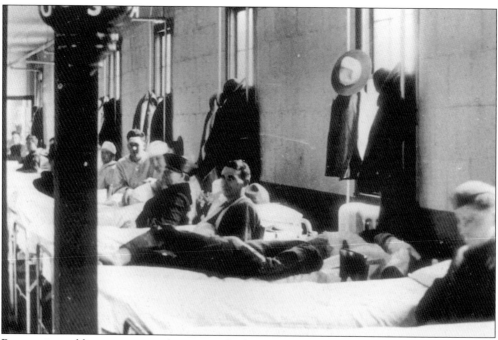

Recovering soldiers are pictured awaiting discharge from the hospital. (Courtesy of National Park Service.)

This group portrait of the medical staff was taken c. 1923. (Courtesy of National Park Service.)

Three medical officers take a few moments to pose atop one of the 8-inch Rodmans—a popular site for photographs to be sent home to families. (Courtesy of National Park Service.)

Nurses of General Hospital No. 2 march into the Star Fort for a ceremony, c. 1920. Baltimore & Ohio Railroad grain warehouses at Locust Point are visible in the background. (Courtesy of National Park Service.)

During World War II, Fort McHenry was used as a U.S. Coast Guard Training Center. Some 28,000 men and women were trained here in port security and shipboard fire prevention. This is a 1943 general view. (Courtesy of National Park Service.)

A Coast Guardsman takes a break by one of the 1837 granite portals of the main gate. (Courtesy of National Park Service.)

Coast Guardsmen march out of the Star Fort following one of many patriotic ceremonies held at the fort during World War II. (Courtesy of National Park Service.)

Four

NATIONAL MONUMENT AND HISTORIC SHRINE

The 1996 aerial view above shows Fort McHenry National Monument and Historic Shrine. (Courtesy of National Park Service.)

The temporary hospital buildings were removed from Fort McHenry in 1927, two years after the post was designated a National Park. In 1939 it was redesignated the nation's only National Monument and Historic Shrine (Courtesy of National Park Service.)

On June 14, 1922, Pres. Warren G. Harding made the first nationwide presidential radio broadcast during ceremonies dedicating classical sculptor Charles Neihaus's Francis Scott Key Monument (Statue of Orpheus). (Courtesy of National Park Service.)

The inscription reads as follows: "To Francis Scott Key, author of The Star-Spangled Banner and to the soldiers and sailors who took part in the Battle of North Point and the defense of Fort McHenry in the War of 1812." (Courtesy of National Park Service.)

This aerial view was taken in 1926, just prior to the demolition of the 140 hospital buildings that surrounded the historic fort. Visible in the middle of the half-circle is the 1922 Key Monument. (Courtesy of National Park Service.)

In 1962 the National Park Service relocated the Key Monument from its original dedication site to another site in the park. It is one of the largest bronze statues in Maryland. (Courtesy of National Park Service.)

Archaeology is an important component of the mission at Fort McHenry. On September 12, 1959—almost exactly the 145th anniversary of the bombardment—archaeologists discovered the original cross-brace timbers that held the base of the original flagstaff from whence the Star-Spangled Banner had flown. (Courtesy of National Park Service.)

In 1982 archaeologists uncovered the remains of a brick traverse wall erected during May 1813 to protect the sally port entrance from an expected British attack. (Courtesy of National Park Service.)

The 1839–1866 gun mount below was recently discovered at Fort McHenry. Many of these structures still remain just beneath the surface in the Star Fort. In 1927 the Army deposited earth fill to cover many of the foundations of the old World War I hospital and Civil War gun mounts. (Courtesy of National Park Service.)

A 1989 archaeological investigation of a Civil War gun mount in the Star Fort shows the remains of the traverse stones for positioning a Model 1842 32-pounder. (Courtesy of National Park Service.)

The original Star-Spangled Banner, which inspired Francis Scott Key, measured 42 by 30 feet. In 1912 the Armistead family donated the flag to the American people and today it is displayed at the Smithsonian's National Museum of American History. (Courtesy of Smithsonian Institution.)

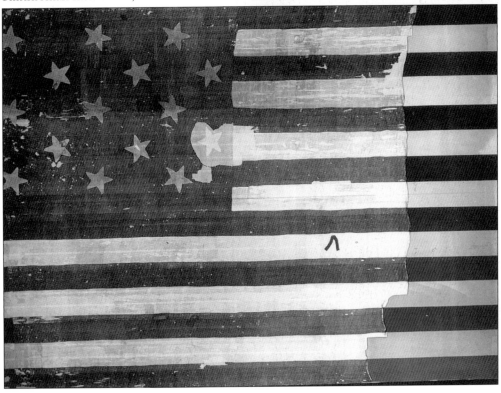

Dale Gallon's *The Flag is Full of Stars*, created in 1989, shows the garrison at the moment the soldiers hoisted the Star-Spangled Banner "o'er the ramparts" on the morning of September 14, 1814. (Courtesy of National Park Service.)

Fort McHenry is seen in 1982 with a replica of the Star-Spangled Banner flying. Only the star-shaped brick walls and first floors are original to 1798; all the other structures were built in the 1830s during Army improvements. (Courtesy of National Park Service.)

Members of the 2nd U.S. Artillery pose formally with a 15-inch Rodman gun during a Civil War living history program in 1983. (Courtesy of National Park Service.)

Superintendent Kayci Cook and First Lady Hillary R. Clinton discuss the recent restoration of the original Star-Spangled Banner while walking along the historic Fort McHenry ramparts in July 1998. Below them post–Civil War artillery keeps a silent vigil over the Patapsco River. (Courtesy of National Park Service.)

Five

FORT CONSTRUCTION AND WEAPONS

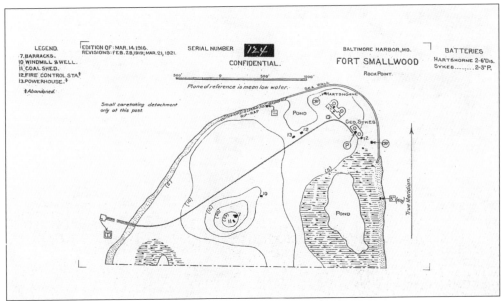

This is a March 1921 fortification plat of Fort Smallwood. The fort's primary mission was to use rapid-fire guns to prevent light draft vessels from clearing minefields. The guns could also be used to drive off landing parties attempting to seize mine casemates or to advance overland on Baltimore. (Courtesy of National Archives.)

THE DEFENSES OF THE HARBOR OF BALTIMORE.

An illustration from the *Baltimore American* of February 28, 1898, is captioned,"Defenses of the Harbor Of Baltimore. A Glance at the Work the Government is Doing on the Fortifications at North Point." (Courtesy of Dundalk-Patapsco Neck Historical Society.)

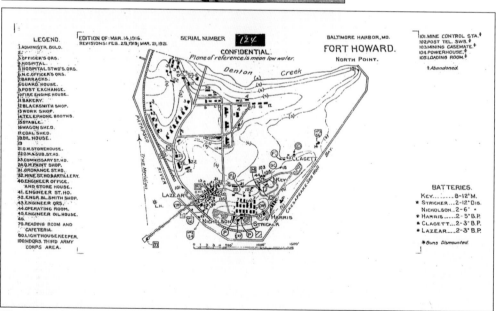

This 1921 fortification plat of Fort Howard shows the batteries and buildings of Baltimore's main harbor defense post. (Courtesy of National Archives.)

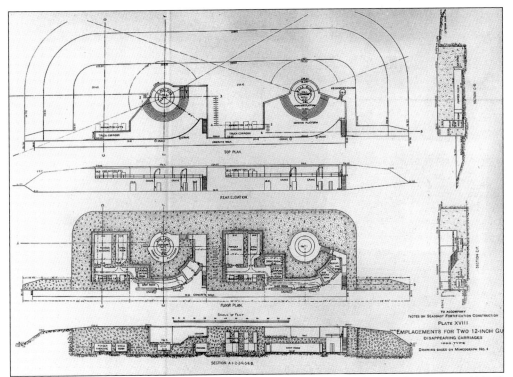

A plate from Col. Eben Eveleth Winslow's *Notes on Seacoast Fortification Construction* (1920) illustrates the design of an 1896 type emplacement for two 12-inch breechloading rifles on disappearing carriages, comparable to the one used to construct Battery Stricker. (Courtesy of Coast Defense Study Group.)

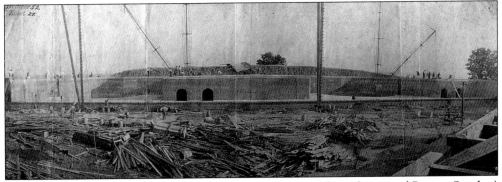

Construction of the dual 12-inch breechloading rifle battery (later designated Battery Stricker) at North Point is seen here on June 30, 1898. This was at the height of the "Spanish Navy raid" scare, when work was proceeding around the clock. (Courtesy of National Archives.)

Here, the construction of the 12-inch breechloading mortar battery (later designated Battery Key) at North Point is shown in 1898. (Courtesy of Dundalk-Patapsco Neck Historical Society.)

In this view of the northeast face of Fort Carroll, old masonry is being removed from the wall for conformance to the new Endicott emplacements. Removed masonry was placed as riprap around the foundations. (Courtesy of Maryland Department, Enoch Pratt Free Library.)

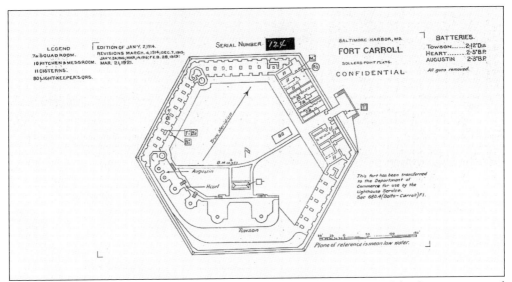

This is the March 1921 fortification plat of Fort Carroll. Construction of the fort was initiated and superintended by Capt. Robert E. Lee. (Courtesy of National Archives.)

Fort Carroll's northeast face is pictured following the construction of concrete emplacements, new ordnance, and fire control facilities. The 60-foot steel tower, at right, supports the primary command station for Battery Towson, with a 40-foot frame secondary mine command station immediately in front. At far left are the 12-inch breechloading rifles of Battery Towson—Fort Carroll's primary armament. Immediately behind the right 12-inch rifle is the lighthouse. The building between the lighthouse and the mine command station is the lightkeeper's residence. (Courtesy of Maryland Department, Enoch Pratt Free Library.)

A 1929 interior view of Fort Carroll, looking toward the junction of the north and northeast faces, shows the power house in the center. (Courtesy of Maryland Department, Enoch Pratt Free Library.)

Seen here is the junction of southwest and southern faces of Fort Carroll with the primary command station for Battery Towson and secondary mine command station on the left; the lighthouse and secondary command stations for Batteries Winchester and McFarland (Fort Armistead) in the center; and Battery Towson on the right. (Courtesy of Maryland Department, Enoch Pratt Free Library.)

This aerial view of Fort Carroll was taken on December 1, 1937, by 104th Observation Section, Maryland National Guard. It shows, in the lower half of the photo (clockwise from right), the empty concrete emplacements for Batteries Towson, Heart, and Augustin. Centered behind Battery Towson is the power house, the lighthouse tower is visible on the southwest face, and the dock off the north face. Squad rooms, kitchen, mess room, and cisterns were situated within the north face. (Courtesy of Maryland Department, Enoch Pratt Free Library.)

This U.S. Army Signal Corps photograph shows the construction of batteries at Hawkins Point on November 30, 1897. Fort Carroll is visible at the far right. (Courtesy of National Archives.)

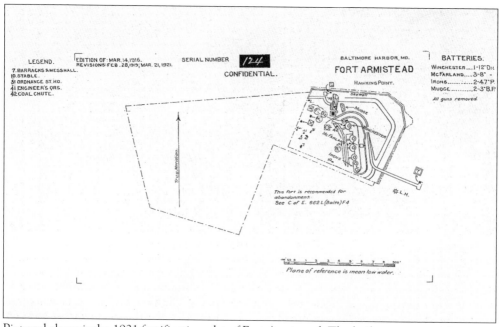

Pictured above is the 1921 fortification plat of Fort Armistead. The built-up area at right is now a city park. (Courtesy of National Archives.)

This is another view of the construction of batteries at Hawkins Point on November 30, 1897. (Courtesy of National Archives.)

The batteries at Hawkins Point (later designated Fort Armistead) are seen here on June 30, 1898. Battery Winchester (one 12-inch breechloading rifle) is at left; Battery McFarland (three 8-inch breechloading rifles) is in the center; and the emplacement for Battery Irons (two 4.7-inch rapid fire guns not yet mounted) is on the right. Construction of Battery Mudge (two 3-inch rapid fire guns) had not begun at the time this photograph was taken; it would be located on the extreme left, beyond Battery Winchester. The background of this photograph—boats on the Patapsco River and absence of Fort Carroll—appears to have been painted on, perhaps for security reasons. (Courtesy of National Archives.)

Heavy caliber guns on disappearing carriages comprised the principal harbor defense armament; their shells were intended to defeat warship armor plating. Armored warships of the era were incapable of high-angle gun elevation, which made effective counterbattery fire impossible. This is a 10-inch breechloading rifled cannon on a disappearing carriage in a reinforced concrete emplacement at Fort Hancock, New Jersey, in July 1894. (Courtesy of National Archives.)

The crew has finished loading and released a restraining pawl, freeing a heavy counterweight to swing the barrel in an arc up and over the parapet into firing position. The gunner is preparing to pull the lanyard to fire the weapon. Recoil will propel the barrel along a reverse path, where the pawl will engage and lock it in position for reloading. (Courtesy of National Archives.)

Above, gunners load one of the paired 12-inch breechloading rifles on disappearing carriages at Fort Howard's Battery Stricker. Projectiles weighed over 1,000 pounds and powder cartridges (carried by soldiers to left of breech) about 80 pounds. (Courtesy of Dundalk-Patapsco Neck Historical Society.)

This breechloading rifle has just been fired and is recoiling back to battery position. (Courtesy of Dundalk-Patapsco Neck Historical Society.)

A "big gun" firing at Fort Howard is pictured in 1912. In training, practice rounds were usually used because the concussion from service ammunition often shattered windows, fractured pipes and seals, caused other damage to the fort, and generated complaints from nearby communities. (Courtesy of Dundalk-Patapsco Neck Historical Society.)

Warship decks were only lightly armored because most defensive artillery could not be significantly elevated. Mortars exploited this weakness by firing high-angle salvos to penetrate vulnerable decks and could also be rotated to fire on enemy landing parties attacking coastal forts from the rear. This 12-inch breechloading mortar pit was photographed at Fort Hancock, New Jersey, in July 1894. (Courtesy of National Archives.)

The 1893 plan for Baltimore harbor defenses called for sixteen 12-inch mortars each at North Point and at Rock Point, a total of 32 pieces. Only one mortar battery was actually built. Battery Key at Fort Howard featured two pits each with four mortars. Gunners are shown posing atop the 12-inch mortars in Pit B. (Courtesy of Dundalk-Patapsco Neck Historical Society.)

Tampions (plugs) were used to keep mortar muzzles dry and clean when not in use. (Courtesy of Dundalk-Patapsco Neck Historical Society.)

These photographs depict Battery Key's mortars being loaded and elevated to firing position. (Courtesy of Dundalk-Patapsco Neck Historical Society.)

Battery Key's mortars are pictured here being fired. The shells on trucks lined up behind the mortars weighed over 1,000 pounds each. (Courtesy of Dundalk-Patapsco Neck Historical Society.)

Fort fire control systems permitted detection, acquisition, tracking, and targeting of enemy warships. This tower was the primary range-finding station for Battery Stricker. To provide redundancy in the event of battle damage or a station being overrun, batteries were provided with secondary and sometimes supplemental stations. (Courtesy of Dundalk-Patapsco Neck Historical Society.)

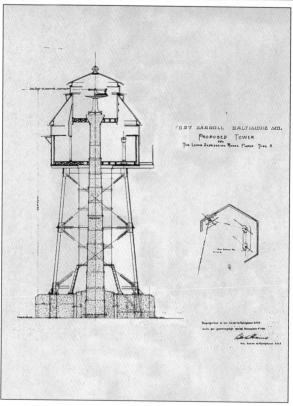

A drawing dated November 9, 1901, shows a proposed fire control tower with Lewis depression range finders for Fort Carroll. (Courtesy of Coast Defense Study Group.)

Mines were used to block ship channels. Most were detonated by an operator in a mining casemate responding to a flashing light signaling that a ship had struck a mine. This photograph, accompanying a report to the Chief of Engineers dated July 22, 1898, is captioned, "Explosion of a triple group of ground mines in Baltimore harbor, July 18th, 1898. Charge 225 to 250 lbs. in each mine. Depth of water 31.5'. Mines had settled in mud so tops were flush with the bottom. Height of tallest column of water 225'." (Courtesy of National Archives.)

This mine (left) is ready for planting, with an anchor (right) to hold it in place. The thick white line is a mooring rope and the thinner dark line is an electrical conductor cable. Cables connected mines in a submarine minefield to the firing casemate ashore. (Courtesy of Coast Defense Study Group.)

The official coat of arms for the Coast Defenses of Baltimore, issued by the U.S. Army Quartermaster General on September 14, 1921, is described as follows: "The shield is the Coat of Arms of the Calvert family, to which Lord Baltimore, the founder of Maryland, belonged. This now forms the 1st and 4th quarters of the arms of the State of Maryland. The chief commemorates the writing of the Star Spangled Banner by Francis Scott Key during the battle of Fort McHenry, September 13, 1814. The flag at that time had fifteen stars and fifteen stripes. The embattled partition line is for the defense of the fortress . . . The translation of the motto is 'with song and deed.'" The crest features a soldier in the uniform of 1812. (Courtesy of U.S. Army Institute of Heraldry.)

Six

FORT HOWARD SCENES AND SOLDIER LIFE

The main gate is seen around 1900. Note the wooden sidewalk and cannon balls atop the gate posts. (Courtesy of Dundalk-Patapsco Neck Historical Society.)

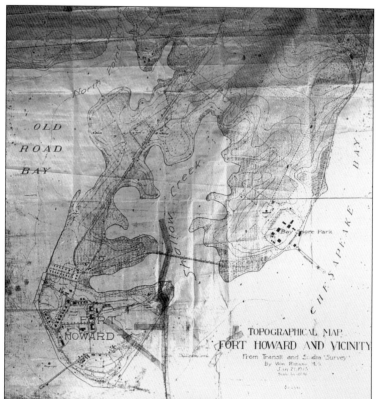

A segment of a Patapsco Neck topographical map is dated January 21, 1913. United Railway and Electric Company operated Bay Shore Park from 1906 to 1947 as a means of generating streetcar fares. Bethlehem Steel purchased the property in 1947 to prevent rival U.S. Steel from acquiring water frontage there. Maryland acquired the property in 1987 and it is now designated North Point State Park. (Courtesy of Dundalk-Patapsco Neck Historical Society.)

Another view shows the main gate, date unknown. (Courtesy of Dundalk-Patapsco Neck Historical Society.)

This photograph was taken from the water tower by G. Waterman in 1907. In the center, tents indicate possible Maryland National Guard coast artillery encampment; on the right are officers' quarters; on the left, post hospital; in left background, enlisted barracks/quarters; and on the upper right and left, trees mask artillery emplacements and pier. (Courtesy of Dundalk-Patapsco Neck Historical Society.)

The enlisted men's barracks were later used as nurses' quarters. (Courtesy of Dundalk-Patapsco Neck Historical Society.)

This view shows the present supply office and warehouse in the foreground. The Veterans Administration hospital was constructed on the central field. (Courtesy of Dundalk-Patapsco Neck Historical Society.)

Some of the horses and mules used for hauling, with stable men, are pictured here, c. 1910. (Courtesy of Dundalk-Patapsco Neck Historical Society.)

"Chow time" is called along the narrow gauge railway used for hauling loaded mines from the mine loading room or storage warehouse to mine planters at the wharf. (Courtesy of Dundalk-Patapsco Neck Historical Society.)

These stewards are ready to serve at the enlisted mess arranged for Thanksgiving dinner, 1912. (Courtesy of Dundalk-Patapsco Neck Historical Society.)

Steamer *Sprigg Carroll* is described in the 1909 Report of the Chief of Coast Artillery as a passenger and freight steamer second class, 110 feet long, used for quartermaster and artillery service within the Artillery District of Baltimore. (Courtesy of Dundalk-Patapsco Neck Historical Society.)

Sprigg Carroll is seen at a wharf in 1920. The flag at her bow is a Quartermaster Corps pennant. (Courtesy of Dundalk-Patapsco Neck Historical Society.)

This soldier in the service uniform of the early 1900s is armed with a Springfield .30-caliber 1903 rifle. (Courtesy of Dundalk-Patapsco Neck Historical Society.)

This soldier is wearing a *c.* 1905 dress uniform. The cap was dark blue with a scarlet stripe and Coast Artillery Corps insignia. The coat was dark blue with a collar, shoulder loops, and cuffs piped in scarlet, a scarlet breast cord, and corps insignia and "U.S." on the standup collar. The trousers are dark blue. The rifle is a Springfield .30-caliber 1903. (Courtesy of Dundalk-Patapsco Neck Historical Society.)

The band poses in full dress uniform in front of the post exchange in 1910. (Courtesy of Dundalk-Patapsco Neck Historical Society.)

A full dress parade at sunset featured precise troop alignments. (Courtesy of Dundalk-Patapsco Neck Historical Society.)

The members of the fort's band are pictured wearing their field uniforms. (Courtesy of Dundalk-Patapsco Neck Historical Society.)

The 103rd Coast Artillery Company marches in a parade, probably in East Baltimore. (Courtesy of Dundalk-Patapsco Historical Society.)

The guard mount is formed at the guardhouse. (Courtesy of Dundalk-Patapsco Neck Historical Society.)

The guard has been formed and is being inspected before posting. (Courtesy of Dundalk-Patapsco Neck Historical Society.)

Soldiers "stand at ease" while the flag is lowered at sunset in 1910. Collar insignia indicate a mix of Regular Army and Maryland National Guard troops. (Courtesy of Dundalk-Patapsco Neck Historical Society.)

This is a group portrait of Coast Artillery Corps officers serving in the Baltimore defenses. (Courtesy of Dundalk-Patapsco Neck Historical Society.)

Soldiers—possibly Maryland National Guardsmen of 1st Coast Artillery Company—polish shoes in front of their tent. (Courtesy of Dundalk-Patapsco Neck Historical Society.)

Soldiers are seen here playing cards in their barracks. (Courtesy of Dundalk-Patapsco Neck Historical Society.)

Military service has always fostered enduring friendships, as evidenced by these soldier buddies. (Courtesy of Dundalk-Patapsco Neck Historical Society.)

This soldier is fishing from the mine wharf in the early 1900s. The narrow gauge railroad for transporting mines from the preparation area to mine planters is visible at left. (Courtesy of Dundalk-Patapsco Neck Historical Society.)

Soldiers relax just outside the Fort Howard gate—"Off the record, off duty, off the reservation." One wag holds aloft a bottle of milk at bottom right. (Courtesy of Dundalk-Patapsco Neck Historical Society.)

Soldiers are seen at leisure after a busy workday. (Courtesy of Dundalk-Patapsco Neck Historical Society.)

Soldiers and their girlfriends are pictured in front of a range finding tower in 1910. (Courtesy of Dundalk-Patapsco Neck Historical Society.)

The Welsh freighter *Alum Chine* exploded off Hawkins Point on the morning of March 7, 1913. The freighter was loading some 350 tons of dynamite for use in the Panama Canal construction. The explosion—which killed 33 seamen, injured about 60 more, and destroyed a tugboat and two barges carrying railroad cars to the ship—was described by a soldier at nearby Fort Armistead as sounding like "the roar of 10,000 cannon." (Courtesy of Maryland Historical Society.)

Soldiers of the 21st Coast Artillery Company lounge in front of their barracks in 1910. (Courtesy of Dundalk-Patapsco Neck Historical Society.)

Coast artillerymen are seen on a practice road march. Artillerymen were required to undergo minimum periods of infantry training each year. (Courtesy of Dundalk-Patapsco Neck Historical Society.)

In this photograph of a field barber shop—located in a tent—the man in the chair is getting a shave. (Courtesy of Dundalk-Patapsco Neck Historical Society.)

Seven

END OF AN ERA

Soldiers enjoyed movies at the Fort Howard post theater. Columbia Pictures released the film advertised here, *Outlaws of the Orient*, in 1937. (Courtesy of Dundalk-Patapsco Neck Historical Society.)

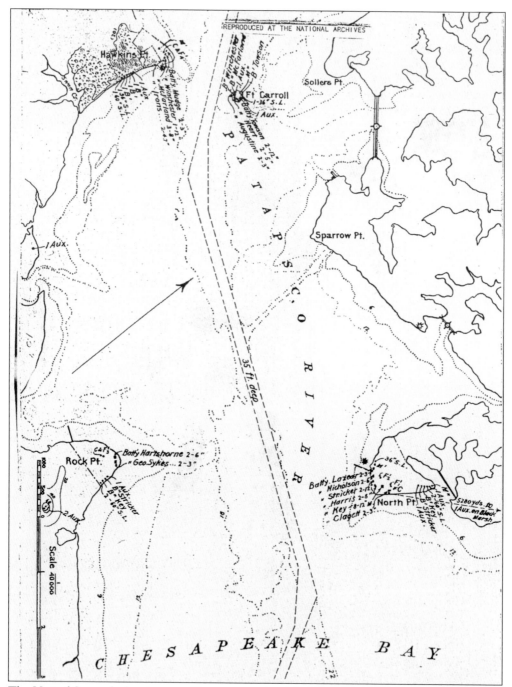

The United States declared war on Germany on April 6, 1917. On May 4, a board convened at
Fort Howard to review the condition of Baltimore's defenses and to recommend improvements.
This map, extracted from the board's official report, indicates each modern battery's armament
and the location of major fire control systems. (Courtesy of National Archives.)

First Battalion, Coast Artillery, Maryland National Guard, was mustered into active federal service for the war on July 25, 1917, and initially assigned to Fort Howard. This photograph shows Maj. J. Carroll Edgar, the battalion's commanding officer. (Courtesy of Maryland Department, Enoch Pratt Free Library)

In addition to serving at Fort Howard, Maryland National Guardsmen were assigned to the 117th Trench Mortar Battery and Battery F, 58th Coast Artillery Regiment. Both units saw combat in France before returning to America in April 1919 to be demobilized. In this 1918 view, Battery F passes a range finding station tower on the way to embark on *Sprigg Carroll* for shipment overseas. (Courtesy of Dundalk-Patapsco Neck Historical Society.)

Ordnance was dismounted from several of Baltimore's forts during the war and shipped to other Army stations, some being forwarded overseas. Here soldiers of 40th Coast Artillery Company are dismounting a 12-inch breechloading rifle at Battery Stricker. The two rifles were dismounted during March and April of 1918 and shipped to Fort Hamilton, New York, on June 14, 1918. (Courtesy of Dundalk-Patapsco Neck Historical Society.)

Fort Howard became an administrative and infantry post following World War I. Maj. Gen. Douglas MacArthur, Third Corps Area Commander, poses with Lt. Col. William P. Screws, 12th Infantry, fort commander, on August 3, 1927. (Courtesy of National Archives.)

MACARTHUR AT FORT HOWARD (AROUND 1927)

MacArthur is seen here addressing the troops, c. 1927. (Courtesy of Dundalk-Patapsco Neck Historical Society.)

The U.S. Army Citizens' Military Training Camp (CMTC) program operated during 1920–1941 to train young men of "high type" for 30 days to promote citizenship, patriotism, and "Americanism." Approximately 30,000 volunteers completed four weeks of military training in summer camps each year. Men who completed four summers became eligible for Reserve second lieutenant commissions. The program was small but remarkably successful in an era of isolationism and pacifism following the "War to End All Wars." Above is a view of CMTC companies parading at Fort Howard on July 6, 1928. (Courtesy of National Archives.)

This view shows the tents of a CMTC encampment. (Courtesy of Dundalk-Patapsco Neck Historical Society.)

Doctors, nurses, and enlisted personnel of a CMTC camp hospital staff are pictured on July 10, 1928. (Courtesy of National Archives.)

Capt. Paul Hathaway, Company D, 12th Infantry, is seen on August 5, 1927 with the trophy and flags won for best CMTC company. (Courtesy of National Archives.)

The U.S. Army was heavily involved in the Civilian Conservation Corps (CCC) program throughout the 1930s. Enrollees were transported to Army bases, examined by medical officers, and given a brief period of physical conditioning and other training before being allocated to field camps to work on conservation projects. This views shows "boys from Baltimore doing practical reforestation work at Fort Howard"—in this instance removing old stumps and filling in the holes under the supervision of a crew foreman. (Courtesy of National Archives.)

Another view shows CCC enrollees at Fort Howard, here "clearing their camp area of unsightly weeds and mosquito breeding places as part of instruction in camp sanitation." (Courtesy of National Archives.)

This aerial view of Fort Howard was taken on April 23, 1932. (Courtesy of Dundalk-Patapsco Neck Historical Society.)

Fort Howard line No. 38 trolley meets Sparrows Point Line No. 26 at Fort Howard junction in the 1930s. Service on the Fort Howard line ended on August 31, 1958. (Courtesy of Dundalk-Patapsco Neck Historical Society.)

This aerial view of the newly constructed Veterans Administration hospital was taken c. 1940. (Courtesy of Dundalk-Patapsco Neck Historical Society.)

Fort Armistead again came to Baltimore's defense early in the Cold War. The Army's Battery A, 35th Antiaircraft Artillery Battalion was located there from 1953 to 1958. A *Baltimore Sun* reporter noted that, in the unlikely event of "enemy ships or submarines moving up to the harbor," the 90-mm. guns could "be lowered, loaded with armor-piercing shells, and brought to bear against them, precisely as the old guns were intended to be used when the fort was first built." Fort Armistead reverted to city park status when Nike surface-to-air missiles replaced tube artillery as primary air defense weapons. Fort Carroll is visible at left center. (Courtesy of the *Baltimore Sun*.)

Among the other units defending Baltimore was the 683rd Antiaircraft Artillery Battalion, activated on November 11, 1955 in the Maryland Army National Guard. The 683rd's distinctive insignia consisted of a shield and motto, officially described as follows: "The scarlet and gold [colors] are used for Artillery. The five-pointed [black] figure represents the 'Star Fort,' Fort McHenry, early defense of the city of Baltimore against hostile attack. The black and gold lower part of the shield is taken from the arms of Calvert, Lord Baltimore. The design refers to the battalion's place of activation and home station of Baltimore, Maryland." The motto, "O'er the Rampart We Watch," alludes to the national anthem. The 683rd later exchanged its 90-mm. guns for Nike missiles, was redesignated the 70th Air Defense Artillery, and served until the air defense program terminated in 1974. In May 1997 this distinctive insignia was officially assigned to the 70th Regiment (Leadership) at Camp Fretterd Military Reservation near Reisterstown. (Courtesy of U.S. Army Institute of Heraldry)

Part of Fort Howard also served during the Cold War. In 1956 the battery area was transferred to the U.S. Army Intelligence School at nearby Fort Holabird, which had no field training area. The school built a "Vietnamese village" called "Duc Huc" on the site and ran a familiarization course for soldiers deploying to Vietnam. The area was deeded to Baltimore County in 1973 for use as a waterfront park. In this view a Special Forces sergeant escorts a "Viet Cong" prisoner through the village gate. (Courtesy of U.S. Army Intelligence and Security Command.)

A column of soldiers from the 5th and 6th Special Forces Groups escorts "Viet Cong" prisoners through the front gate. Although this photo series is undated, the weapons and uniforms suggest it was taken in 1963–1964. (Courtesy of U.S. Army Intelligence and Security Command.)

These Special Forces soldiers are engaged in intelligence training at "Duc Huc." (Courtesy of U.S. Army Intelligence and Security Command.)

Eight
THE FORTS TODAY

An aerial view from the northeast shows Fort Smallwood's Battery Hartshorne in the foreground and Fort Howard, identifiable by the white water tower in right center distance, across the Patapsco River. (Courtesy of Merle T. Cole.)

Battery Hartshorn at Fort Smallwood Park is seen in this aerial view. Battery George Sykes, demolished sometime after 1921, stood just outside the picture where the roadway curves to the right. (Courtesy of Merle T. Cole)

This is the view seen when approaching Battery Hartshorne from the rear. (Courtesy of Merle T. Cole.)

This aerial view of Fort Armistead Park, looking south, shows (clockwise from bottom left) a parking lot, the docks on the Patapsco River, the Millennium Inorganic Chemicals plant, the fort access road, and the park access road. In the center are artillery batteries (from top to bottom) Irons, McFarland, and Winchester. On the north side of the park access road, across from Battery Winchester, are barely discernable remains of Battery Mudge. The mining casemate is located in the rear face of the hill in the lower right corner. (Courtesy of Merle T. Cole.)

Another aerial view of Fort Armistead Park, looking north, shows the Francis Scott Key Bridge at top left. The Key Bridge opened to traffic in March 1977. (Courtesy of Merle T. Cole.)

Battery McFarland, Fort Armistead, is seen from the fort access road. The power plant, defaced by graffiti, is in the center. Concrete steps and a footbridge both lead to the battery loading platform. (Courtesy of Merle T. Cole.)

Pictured above are the Battery McFarland canopies and corridor. Just visible in the shadows of the near canopy are openings to receiving tables where ammunition and propellant charges were delivered from magazines within the battery. (Courtesy of Merle T. Cole.)

Looking north along the Fort Armistead access road, Battery Irons is seen on the right and Battery McFarland on the left. (Courtesy of Merle T. Cole.)

The Francis Scott Key bridge, carrying I-695, towers beyond the Fort Armistead Park parking lot. (Courtesy of Merle T. Cole.)

This is the view seen when approaching Fort Armistead from the rear. Trees planted as camouflage actually made some battery sites more conspicuous when viewed from the water. (Courtesy of Merle T. Cole.)

This aerial view of Fort Carroll was taken in the summer of 1976 and shows the construction of the Key Bridge. (Courtesy of Baltimore County Public Library.)

Above, a 1992 aerial view of Fort Carroll looks southwest across Battery Towson. (Courtesy of Merle T. Cole.)

The northeast face of Fort Carroll is seen here, with the center span of Francis Scott Key Bridge in the background. (Courtesy of Merle T. Cole.)

Pictured is the landing dock at Fort Carroll, with the lighthouse at right. (Courtesy of Merle T. Cole.)

An aerial view of Fort Howard shows, clockwise from bottom center, the sea wall along the Chesapeake Bay, artillery batteries in park woods, the pier, the lighthouse, the grounds of the Veterans Hospital, the Patapsco River, Old Road Bay (the site of the British landing in 1814), the water tower, Denton Creek, and the park access road. (Courtesy of Merle T. Cole.)

This aerial view of Fort Howard looks toward the southern end of the park. Visible batteries are, from top center, Nicholson (two 6-inch breechloading rifles), Stricker (two 12-inch breechloading rifles), and Harris (two 5-inch rapid fire guns). Battery Lazear (two 3-inch rapid fire guns) was located to the right of the building at the end of the pier before being demolished sometime after 1941. (Courtesy of Merle T. Cole)

This view of Fort Howard looks northeast along Patapsco Neck, with the Veterans Hospital grounds prominent in the center. (Courtesy of Merle T. Cole.)

This view was captured from Battery Stricker's loading platform looking down into the gun platform. The chain link fence was mounted atop the blast apron as a park safety feature. (Courtesy of Merle T. Cole.)

This access road is located behind Battery Stricker. Shell rooms, magazines, tool rooms, and other work areas located within the battery could be entered from this road. (Courtesy of Merle T. Cole.)

This electric plant powered Fort Howard's searchlights. It is located behind Battery Stricker. (Courtesy of Merle T. Cole.)

Pictured here is Battery Harris's observation and fire control post. (Courtesy of Merle T. Cole.)

This rear view of a Battery Key mortar pit shows a data booth for transmitting firing directions at left. (Courtesy of Merle T. Cole.)

The main fort power plant behind Battery Key was converted to restrooms. (Courtesy of Merle T. Cole.)

The mining casemate in the rear of Battery Key is now closed off with steel shutters. Insulated cables led from the casemate to mines anchored in the Chesapeake Bay and Patapsco River. (Courtesy of Merle T. Cole.)

Pictured here is the view approaching Battery Clagett from the rear. (Courtesy of Merle T. Cole.)

The remains of a quarters building illustrate an early use of preformed concrete construction. The "Duc Huc" Vietnamese village was built in the nearby woods. (Courtesy of Merle T. Cole.)

REFERENCES

Cole, Merle T. "Defending Baltimore During the 'Splendid Little War.' " *Maryland Historical Magazine* 93 (Summer 1998): 158–181.

———. "Fort Armistead." *Anne Arundel County* [MD] *History News* 25 (July 1994): 1–2, 8–11.

———. "Fort Carroll." *Anne Arundel County* [MD] *History News* 26 (Oct. 1994): 1, 4, 6, 9–12.

———. "Fort Howard's 'Vietnamese Village.' " *Coast Defense Study Group Journal* 7 (Spring 1993): 10–12.

———. "Fort Smallwood's Military Mission." *Anne Arundel County* [MD] *History News* 25 (Apr. 1994): 1, 6, 8, 9–11.

———. "Imperial German Invasion Plans and Landward Defense of the Patapsco River Forts." *Coast Defense Study Group Journal* 7 (Fall 1993): 31–43.

———. "Maryland National Guard Coast Artillery, 1908–1917." *Military Collector and Historian* 45 (Summer 1993): 50-62.

Lewis, Emanuel Raymond. *Seacoast Fortifications of the United States: An Introductory History.* Annapolis: Naval Institute Press, 1993.

Sheads, Scott S. *Baltimore During the Civil War.* Baltimore: Toomey Press, 1997.

———. *Fort McHenry: A History.* Baltimore: Nautical & Aviation Pub., 1995.

———. *Fort McHenry: Home of the Brave.* Santa Barbara, CA: Sequoia Comm., 1989.

———. *Guardian of the Star-Spangled Banner: Major George Armistead and the Fort McHenry Flag.* Baltimore: Toomey Press, 1999.

———. *The Rockets' Red Glare: The Maritime Defense of Baltimore in 1814.* Centreville, MD: Tidewater Pub., 1986.